LAW ON LAWYERS

Essential Legal Terms Explained You Need To Know About Law on Lawyers!

DR. PETER JOHNSON

Copyright © 2019

All rights reserved.

ISBN: 9781090114884

TEXT COPYRIGHT © [DR. PETER JOHNSON]

all rights reserved. No part of this guide may be reproduced in any form without permission in writing from the publisher except in the case of brief quotations embodied in critical articles or reviews.

Legal & disclaimer

The information contained in this book and its contents is not designed to replace or take the place of any form of medical or professional advice; and is not meant to replace the need for independent medical, financial, legal or other professional advice or services, as may be required. The content and information in this book have been provided for educational and entertainment purposes only.

The content and information contained in this book have been compiled from sources deemed reliable, and it is accurate to the best of the author's knowledge, information, and belief. However, the author cannot guarantee its accuracy and validity and cannot be held liable for any errors and/or omissions. Further, changes are periodically made to this book as and when needed. Where appropriate and/or necessary, you must consult a professional (including but not limited to your doctor, attorney, financial advisor or such other professional advisor) before using any of the suggested remedies, techniques, or information in this book.

Upon using the contents and information contained in this book, you agree to hold harmless the author from and against any damages, costs, and expenses, including any legal fees potentially resulting from the application of any of the information provided by this book. This disclaimer applies to any loss, damages or injury caused by the use and application, whether directly or indirectly, of any advice or information presented, whether for breach of contract, tort, negligence, personal injury, criminal intent, or under any other cause of action.

You agree to accept all risks of using the information presented inside this book.

You agree that by continuing to read this book, where appropriate and/or necessary, you shall consult a professional (including but not limited to your doctor, attorney, or financial advisor or such other advisor as needed) before using any of the suggested remedies, techniques, or information in this book.

Table of Contents

Introduction

Lawyers

Social Functions Of Lawyers

Legal Services Provided By Lawyers

Principles For Law Practice

Principles For Management Of Law Practice

Socio-Professional Organizations Of Lawyers

Encouragement Of Pro Bono Legal Aid

Prohibited Acts

Criteria Of Lawyers

Lawyer Training

Persons Exempt From Lawyer Training

Law Practice Probation

Grant Of Law Practice Certificates

Joining Bar Associations

Rights And Obligations Of Lawyers

Law Practice

Forms Of Law Practice By Lawyers

Acceptance And Settlement Of Clients' Cases Or Affairs

Confidentiality

[Provision Of Legal Services Under Legal Service Contracts](#)

[Lawyers' Participation In Legal Proceedings](#)

[Legal Consultancy Activities Of Lawyers](#)

[Lawyers' Representation Beyond Legal Proceedings](#)

[Other Legal Services Provided By Lawyers](#)

[Pro Bono Legal Aid Provided By Lawyers](#)

[Forms Of Law-Practicing Organizations](#)

[Lawyer's Office](#)

[Law Firm](#)

[Registration Of Operations Of Law-Practicing Organizations](#)

[Rights Of A Law-Practicing Organization](#)

[Obligations Of A Law-Practicing Organization](#)

[Transaction Offices Of Law-Practicing Organizations](#)

[Nomination Of Lawyers To Provide Legal Services In Foreign Countries](#)

[Lawyers Practicing Law Individually](#)

[Rights And Obligations Of Lawyers Practicing Law Individually Under Legal Service Contracts](#)

[Rights And Obligations Of Lawyers Practicing Law Individually Under Labor Contracts](#)

[Lawyers' Remunerations](#)

[Grounds And Modes Of Calculating Remunerations](#)

Remunerations And Expenses For Lawyers Who Provide Legal Services Under Legal Service Contracts

Remunerations And Expenses For Lawyers Who Participate In Legal Proceedings At The Request Of Legal Proceeding-Conducting Agencies

Wages For Lawyers Practicing Law Individually Under Labor Contracts

Settlement Of Disputes Over Remunerations, Expenses And Wages Under Labor Contracts

Bar Association

Tasks And Powers Of A Bar Association

National Lawyers' Organization

Tasks And Powers Of The National Lawyers' Organization

Discipline Of Lawyers

Complaint About Disciplinary Decisions Against Lawyers

Complaint About Decisions Or Acts Of The Managing Boards Of Bar Associations Or Bodies Of The National Lawyers' Organization

Settlement Of Disputes

Handling Of Violations Of Lawyers

Handling Of Acts Of Infringing Upon Legitimate Rights And Interests Of Lawyers And Law-Practicing Organizations

Handling Of Violations Of Individuals And Organizations That Illegally Practice Law

Conclusion

Check Out Other Books

Introduction

Thank you and congratulate you for downloading the book *"LAW ON LAWYERS: Essential Legal Terms Explained You Need To Know About Law on Lawyers!"*

With a clear, concise, and engaging writing style, Dr. Peter Johnson will help you with a practical understanding of lawyer law topics about social functions of lawyers, principles for law practice, criteria of lawyers, lawyer training, law practice, lawyers' participation in legal proceedings, legal consultancy activities of lawyers, lawyers' representation beyond legal proceedings, lawyers' remunerations, bar association; provide you a road map to navigating law on lawyers rules and help you build a foundation for understanding the overall picture and much much more. This book delivers extensive coverage of every aspect of the law and details the duties a paralegal is expected to perform when working within law on lawyers. High-level, comprehensive coverage is combined with cutting-edge developments and foundational concepts.

As the author of the book, I promise this book will be an invaluable source of legal reference for professionals, international lawyers, law students, business professionals and anyone else who want to improve their use of legal terminology, succinct clarification of legal terms and have a better understanding of law on lawyers. All legal terms and phrases are well written and explained clearly in plain English.

Thank you again for purchasing this book, and I hope you enjoy it.

Let's get started!

LAWYERS

Lawyers are persons who fully the meet the criteria and conditions for professional practice under the provisions of Law on lawyers and provide legal services at the request of individuals, agencies or organizations (hereinafter collectively referred to as clients).

SOCIAL FUNCTIONS OF LAWYERS

Legal professional activities aim at contributing to the protection of justice, the economic development and the building of an equitable, democratic and civilized society.

LEGAL SERVICES PROVIDED BY LAWYERS

Legal services provided by lawyers include participation in legal proceedings, provision of legal consultancy, representation of clients beyond legal proceedings and other legal services.

PRINCIPLES FOR LAW PRACTICE

1. Observance of the Constitution and law.

2. Observance of the rules on legal professional ethics and conducts.

3. Independence, honesty and respect for objective truths.

4. Use of lawful measures for the best protection of clients' legitimate rights and interests.

5. Accountability before law for law-practicing activities.

PRINCIPLES FOR MANAGEMENT OF LAW PRACTICE

The management of law practice shall comply with the principle of combining the state management with the promotion of self-control of socio-professional organizations of lawyers, ensuring the observance of law and the rules of legal professional ethics and conducts.

SOCIO-PROFESSIONAL ORGANIZATIONS OF LAWYERS

Socio-professional organizations of lawyers are set up to represent lawyers and protect their legitimate rights and interests, provide professional training and retraining for lawyers, oversee lawyers in their observance of law and rules of professional ethics and conducts, and manage law practice in accordance with Law on lawyers.

Socio-professional organizations of lawyers include bar associations in provinces and centrally run cities and the national lawyers' organization.

ENCOURAGEMENT OF PRO BONO LEGAL AID

The State encourages lawyers and law-practicing organizations to provide pro bono legal aid.

PROHIBITED ACTS

1. Lawyers are forbidden to commit the following acts:

a/ Providing legal services to clients who have conflicting interests in the same criminal, civil or administrative case or civil affair (hereinafter collectively referred to as cases and affairs) as provided for by law;

b/ Intentionally supplying forged or untruthful documents or material evidences; instigating detainees, the accused, defendants or involved persons to make untruthful declarations or instigating clients to make complaints, denunciations or petitions in contravention of law;

c/ Disclosing information on cases, affairs or clients they have acquired in the process of professional practice, unless it is agreed by clients in writing or otherwise provided for by law.

d/ Harassing or deceiving clients;

e/ Receiving or asking for any money amounts or benefits other than remunerations and charges agreed upon with clients in legal service contracts;

f/ Establishing contacts or relations with persons conducting or participating in legal proceedings or with cadres or civil servants to act in contravention of law in the settlement of cases or affairs;

g/ Abusing law practice or the lawyer's title to cause harms to national security, social order or safety, infringing upon the State's interests, public interests or legitimate rights and interests of agencies, organizations or individuals.

2. Agencies, organizations and individuals may not commit acts of obstructing lawyers from practicing their profession.

CRITERIA OF LAWYERS

Citizens who are loyal to the Fatherland, observe the Constitution and law, have good moral qualities, possess a law bachelor diploma, have been trained in legal profession, have gone through the probation of legal profession and have good health for law practice may become lawyers.

LAWYER TRAINING

1. A person who possesses a law bachelor diploma may register to participate in a lawyer-training course at a lawyer-training establishment.

2. A person who completes the lawyer-training program shall be granted a graduation certificate by the concerned lawyer-training establishment.

3. The Government shall provide for lawyer-training establishments.

PERSONS EXEMPT FROM LAWYER TRAINING

1. Those who have been judges, procurators or investigators.

2. Professors, associate professors of law; doctors of law.

3. Those who have been senior court examiners; senior procuracy inspectors; senior legal experts, researchers or lecturers.

4. Those who have been principal court examiners or principal procuracy inspectors; principal legal experts, researchers or lecturers.

LAW PRACTICE PROBATION

1. Persons who possess lawyer-training certificates may take probation at law-practicing organizations.

Law-practicing organizations shall assign lawyers to guide probationers in the practice of law.

2. Law probationers shall register their probation with the bar associations of localities where law-practicing organizations in which they are taking probation are based.

Bar associations shall oversee the observance of the Regulation on law practice probation.

3. Law probationers may assist instructing lawyers in professional activities; must neither accept nor provide legal services for clients.

4. Upon the expiration of the probation period, instructing lawyers shall give written comments on probation results of probationers and send those comments to the bar associations where they register their probation.

GRANT OF LAW PRACTICE CERTIFICATES

Persons who pass law practice-probation tests shall file dossiers of application for law practice certificates with the managing boards of the bar associations where they register their probation. A dossier of application for such a certificate comprises:

a/ An application for a law practice certificate;

b/ A curriculum vitae;

c/ A judicial record card;

d/ A copy of the law bachelor or master diploma;

e/ A copy of the lawyer-training certificate;

f/ A copy of the law practice-probation certificate;

g/ A health certificate.

Within 7 working days after receiving a complete dossier, the managing board of the concerned bar association shall send, together with the dossier, a written proposal for the grant of a law practice certificate to the Justice Ministry.

JOINING BAR ASSOCIATIONS

1. A person who possesses a law practice certificate may join a bar association of his/her choice for law practice.

2. A person who possesses a law practice certificate shall send a dossier for joining a bar association to that association's managing board. Such a dossier comprises:

a/ A written registration of joining the bar association;

b/ A curriculum vitae;

c/ A copy of the law practice certificate;

d/ A legal record card;

e/ A health certificate.

RIGHTS AND OBLIGATIONS OF LAWYERS

1. Lawyers have the following rights:

a/ To practice law, to select forms of law practice and forms of law-practicing organization in accordance with the Law;

b/ To practice law;

c/ To practice law overseas;

d/ Other rights as provided for by Law.

2. Lawyers have the following obligations:

a/ To observe the law practice principles;

b/ To take lawful measures to protect legitimate rights and interests of their clients;

c/ To participate in legal proceedings in cases at the request of legal proceeding-conducting agencies.

d/ To provide pro bono legal aid;

e/ Other obligations as provided for by Law on lawyers.

LAW PRACTICE

1. Participating in legal proceedings as defense counsels for detainees, the accused or defendants or as defenders of interests of victims, claimants or respondents in civil cases, or of people with related interests and obligations in criminal cases.

2. Participating in legal proceedings as representatives or defenders of legitimate rights and interests of claimants, respondents, persons with related rights and obligations in civil disputes, marriage and family, business, commercial, labor or administrative cases or affairs as well as in other cases and affairs specified by law.

3. Providing legal consultancy.

4. Representing clients beyond legal proceedings in order to carry out related legal tasks.

5. Providing other legal services in accordance with the Law.

FORMS OF LAW PRACTICE BY LAWYERS

1. Practicing law in a law-practicing organization.

A lawyer may practice law in a law-practicing organization by establishing or joining in the establishment of the law-practicing organization or working for the law-practicing organization under a contract.

2. Practicing law individually.

ACCEPTANCE AND SETTLEMENT OF CLIENTS' CASES OR AFFAIRS

1. Lawyers shall respect clients' selection of lawyers; shall only accept cases and affairs suitable with their capabilities and settle them within the scope of the clients' requests.

2. When accepting cases or affairs, lawyers shall notify their clients of their rights, obligations and professional liabilities in the provision of legal services to clients.

3. Unless it is consented by clients or in force majeure circumstances, lawyers may not transfer cases or affairs they have accepted to others.

CONFIDENTIALITY

1. Unless it is consented by clients in writing or otherwise provided for by law, lawyers may not disclose information on cases, affairs or clients they know in the course of professional practice.

2. Lawyers may not use information on cases, affairs or clients they know in professional practice for the purpose of infringing upon the State's interests, public interests or legitimate rights and interests of agencies, organizations or individuals.

3. Law-practicing organizations shall ensure that their staff members do not disclose information on their cases, affairs or clients.

PROVISION OF LEGAL SERVICES UNDER LEGAL SERVICE CONTRACTS

1. Lawyers shall provide legal services under legal service contracts, except for those who participate in legal proceedings at the request of legal proceeding-conducting agencies and those who practice law individually under labor contracts with agencies or organizations.

2. Legal service contracts must be made in writing with the following principal contents:

a/ Names and addresses of the client or his/her representative and of the representative of the law-practicing organization or the lawyer practicing law individually;

b/ Service contents and contract performance duration;

c/ Rights and obligations of the involved parties;

d/ The mode of calculation of remuneration and specific remuneration levels; expenses (if any);

e/ Liabilities incurred upon a breach of the contract.

f/ The mode of settlement of disputes.

LAWYERS' PARTICIPATION IN LEGAL PROCEEDINGS

1. Lawyers' participation in legal proceedings shall comply with the procedural law and Law on lawyers.

2. When fully producing papers in one of the following cases, a lawyer may be granted by the legal proceeding-conducting agency a certificate of defense counsel, certificate of defender of interests of an involved party in a criminal case or certificate of defender of legitimate rights and interests of an involved party in a civil affair or administrative case (hereinafter collectively referred to as lawyer's certificate of participation in legal proceedings):

a/ The lawyer's card, the client's written request for a lawyer and the introduction paper of the law-practicing organization or its branch where the lawyer practices law, in case such lawyer practices law in a law-practicing organization;

b/ The lawyer's card, the client's written request for a lawyer and the introduction paper of the bar association of which the lawyer is a member, in case he/she practices law individually; the lawyer's card and the introduction paper of the agency or organization where the lawyer practices law individually under a labor contract in order to protect legitimate rights and interests of that agency or organization;

c/ The lawyer's card and the document on lawyer nomination by a law-practicing organization or its branch where he/she practices law, for the lawyer who practices law in a law-practicing organization, or the lawyer's card and the document of lawyer nomination by the bar association, for the lawyer who practices law individually, in order to participate in legal proceedings in a criminal case at the request of the legal proceeding-conducting agency.

LEGAL CONSULTANCY ACTIVITIES OF LAWYERS

1. Legal consultancy means that lawyers guide, give opinions to or assist their clients in drafting papers related to the exercise of the latter's rights or the performance of the latter's obligations.

Lawyers may provide legal consultancy in all fields of law.

2. When providing legal consultancy, lawyers shall assist their clients in strictly observing law in order to protect the latter's legitimate rights and interests.

LAWYERS' REPRESENTATION BEYOND LEGAL PROCEEDINGS

1. Lawyers may represent their clients in settling affairs related to the jobs they have taken within the scope and according to the contents of the legal service contracts or as assigned by agencies or organizations for which they practice law individually under labor contracts.

2. When representing their clients, lawyers have the rights and obligations as provided for by relevant laws.

OTHER LEGAL SERVICES PROVIDED BY LAWYERS

1. Other legal services provided by lawyers include assisting clients in performing jobs related to administrative procedures; providing legal advice in case of settlement of complaints; translating, certifying papers and transactions and assisting clients in performing other jobs in accordance with law.

2. When providing other legal services, lawyers have the rights and obligations as provided for by relevant laws.

PRO BONO LEGAL AID PROVIDED BY LAWYERS

1. When providing pro bono legal aid, lawyers must be devoted to the legal aid-receivers as to their clients in charged cases and affairs.

2. Lawyers shall provide pro bono legal aid according to the charter of the national lawyers' organization.

FORMS OF LAW-PRACTICING ORGANIZATIONS

1. Forms of law-practicing organizations include:

a/ Lawyers' offices;

b/ Law firms.

2. Law-practicing organizations are organized and operate under the provisions of Law on lawyers and other relevant provisions of law.

3. A lawyer may only establish, or join in the establishment of, one law-practicing organization in the locality where exists a bar association of which he/she is a member. Where lawyers of different bar associations jointly set up a law firm, they may opt to establish it and register its operations in the locality where exists the bar association of which one of them is a member.

LAWYER'S OFFICE

1. A lawyer's office set up by a lawyer is organized and operates in the form of a private enterprise.

The lawyer who sets up a lawyer's office is the chief of the office and takes charge of fulfilling all the office's obligations with all his/her property. The chief of an office is the office's representative at law.

2. The name of a lawyer's office is selected by the lawyer according to the provisions of the Enterprise Law but must contain the phrase "lawyer's office", must not be identical to, or cause confusion with, the names of registered law-practicing organizations and must not contain words, phrases or symbols against the historical, cultural or ethical traditions as well as fine customs of the nation.

3. A lawyer's office has its own seal and account as provided for by law.

LAW FIRM

1. Law firms include law partnerships and limited liability law firms. Law firms' members must be lawyers.

2. A law partnership must be set up by at least two lawyers. Law partnerships do not have capital-contributing members.

3. Limited liability law firms include limited liability law firms with two or more members and one-member limited liability law firms.

A limited liability law firm with two or more members must be set up by at least two lawyers.

A one-member limited liability law firm is set up by one lawyer who is also the owner of the firm.

4. Members of a law partnership or limited liability law firm with two or more members shall reach agreement to nominate one of them to be the firm's director. The lawyer who owns a one-member limited liability law firm is the firm's director.

5. The names of law partnerships or limited liability law firms with two or more members shall be selected and agreed upon by all members; the names of one-member limited liability law firms shall be selected by the firms' owners in accordance with the Enterprise Law, which, however, must contain the phrase " law partnership" or " limited liability law firm", must not be identical to, or cause confusion with, the names of other registered law-practicing organizations, and must not contain words, phrases or symbols against the historical, cultural or ethical traditions as well as fine customs of the nation.

REGISTRATION OF OPERATIONS OF LAW-PRACTICING ORGANIZATIONS

1. A law-practicing organization shall register its operations at the provincial/municipal Justice Service of the locality where exists the bar association of which the chief of the lawyer's office or the director of the law firm is a member. A law firm jointly set up by lawyers of different bar associations shall register its operations at the provincial/municipal Justice Service of the locality where the firm is based.

2. Law-practicing organizations shall send operation registration dossiers to the provincial/municipal Justice Services. Such a dossier comprises:

a/ A written request for operation registration, made according to a set form;

b/ A draft charter of the law firm;

c/ Copies of the law practice certificate and lawyer's card of the lawyer who sets up the lawyer's office, sets up or joins in setting up the law firm.

d/ Papers evidencing the headquarters of the law-practicing organization.

3. Within 10 working days after receiving a complete dossier, the provincial/municipal Justice Service shall grant an operation registration paper to the law-practicing organization; in case of refusal, it shall give written notice, clearly stating the reasons therefor and the person who is not granted that paper may lodge a complaint in accordance with law.

4. A law-practicing organization may start operation on the date it is granted the operation registration paper.

Within 7 working days after being granted the operation registration paper, the chief of the lawyer's office or the director of the law firm shall give a written notice together with a copy of the operation registration paper to the bar association of which he/she is a member.

RIGHTS OF A LAW-PRACTICING ORGANIZATION

1. To provide legal services;

2. To receive remunerations from its clients.

3. To hire lawyers to work for it.

4. To cooperate with foreign law-practicing organizations.

5. To set up local branches or transaction offices.

6. To locate its practicing establishments overseas.

7. Other rights as provided for by Law on lawyers and relevant laws.

OBLIGATIONS OF A LAW-PRACTICING ORGANIZATION

1. To operate only in the practice domains stated in its operation registration paper.

2. To fulfill its commitments to clients.

3. To nominate its lawyers to participate in legal proceedings according to the assignment of the bar association.

4. To create conditions for its lawyers to provide pro bono legal aid.

5. To pay compensation for damage caused by its lawyers to its clients in legal consultancy provision, in representation beyond legal proceedings or in the provision of other legal services.

6. To purchase professional liability insurance for its lawyers in accordance with the insurance business law.

7. To observe the labor, tax, financial and statistical laws.

8. To abide by the competent state agencies' requests for reporting, inspection or examination.

9. Other obligations as provided for by Law on lawyers and relevant laws.

TRANSACTION OFFICES OF LAW-PRACTICING ORGANIZATIONS

The transaction office of a law-practicing organization may be set up within a province or centrally-run city where that organization registers its operations. The transaction office is the place to receive cases, affairs and requests of clients. It may not provide legal services.

Within 5 working days after setting up a transaction office, a law-practicing organization shall notify in writing the transaction office's address to the provincial/municipal Justice Service of the locality where it registers its operations.

The provincial/municipal Justice Service shall write the address of the transaction office of the law-practicing organization in its operation registration certificate.

NOMINATION OF LAWYERS TO PROVIDE LEGAL SERVICES IN FOREIGN COUNTRIES

Law-practicing organizations may nominate lawyers to provide legal services in foreign countries at the request of their clients.

Lawyers who provide legal services in foreign countries shall observe the provisions of Law on lawyers and relevant laws.

LAWYERS PRACTICING LAW INDIVIDUALLY

1. Lawyers practicing law individually are those who personally accept cases or affairs and provide legal services to their clients, take responsibility for their professional practice with all their property and operate in the form of private business households.

Lawyers practicing law individually may each register only one transaction place and have no seals.

2. Lawyers shall practice law individually by providing legal services for clients under legal service contracts or working for agencies or organizations under labor contracts.

RIGHTS AND OBLIGATIONS OF LAWYERS PRACTICING LAW INDIVIDUALLY UNDER LEGAL SERVICE CONTRACTS

1. Lawyers practicing law individually under legal service contracts have the following rights:

a/ To provide legal services;

b/ To receive remunerations from clients;

c/ Other rights as provided for by Law on lawyers and relevant laws.

2. Lawyers practicing law individually under legal service contracts have the following obligations:

a/ To operate only in the professional domains stated in their law practice-registration papers;

b/ To strictly implement the contents of legal service contracts concluded with clients;

c/ To pay compensations for damage caused to clients due to their faults in the provision of legal consultancy, representation beyond legal proceedings or in the provision of other legal services;

d/ To purchase professional liability insurance in accordance with the insurance business law;

e/ To observe the tax, financial and statistical laws;

f/ To abide by the competent state agencies' requests on reporting, inspection and examination;

g/ Other obligations as provided for by Law on lawyers and relevant laws.

RIGHTS AND OBLIGATIONS OF LAWYERS PRACTICING LAW INDIVIDUALLY UNDER LABOR CONTRACTS

1. Lawyers practicing law individually under labor contracts may provide legal services according to the contents of labor contracts concluded with agencies or organizations.

2. The rights and obligations of lawyers practicing law individually under labor contracts, of agencies and organizations hiring those lawyers shall comply with the labor law, Law on lawyers and relevant laws.

LAWYERS' REMUNERATIONS

Clients shall pay remunerations for legal services provided by lawyers. The receipt of remunerations shall comply with Law on lawyers and relevant laws.

GROUNDS AND MODES OF CALCULATING REMUNERATIONS

1. Remuneration levels are calculated on the following grounds:

a/ Contents and characteristics of legal services;

b/ Time and labor spent by lawyers on the provision of legal services;

c/ Experience and prestige of lawyers.

2. Remunerations are calculated by the following modes:

a/ Working hours of lawyers;

b/ Cases or affairs with package remunerations;

c/ Cases or affairs with remunerations calculated in percentages of the threshold costs of lawsuits or the value of contracts or projects;

d/ Long-term contracts with fixed remunerations.

REMUNERATIONS AND EXPENSES FOR LAWYERS WHO PROVIDE LEGAL SERVICES UNDER LEGAL SERVICE CONTRACTS

1. Remuneration levels shall be agreed upon in legal service contracts; for criminal cases where lawyers participate in legal proceedings, remuneration levels shall not exceed the ceiling level set by the Government.

2. Traveling, accommodation and other reasonable expenses for the provision of legal services shall be agreed upon by the concerned parties in legal service contracts.

REMUNERATIONS AND EXPENSES FOR LAWYERS WHO PARTICIPATE IN LEGAL PROCEEDINGS AT THE REQUEST OF LEGAL PROCEEDING-CONDUCTING AGENCIES

Lawyers who participate in legal proceedings at the request of legal proceeding-conducting agencies are entitled to remunerations and expenses according to the Government's regulations.

WAGES FOR LAWYERS PRACTICING LAW INDIVIDUALLY UNDER LABOR CONTRACTS

Lawyers practicing law individually for agencies or organizations under labor contracts are entitled to wages as agreed upon in the labor contracts.

The agreement on and payment of wages shall comply with the labor law.

SETTLEMENT OF DISPUTES OVER REMUNERATIONS, EXPENSES AND WAGES UNDER LABOR CONTRACTS

1. The settlement of disputes over remunerations and expenses for lawyers shall comply with the civil law.

2. The settlement of disputes over wages for lawyers practicing law individually under labor contracts with agencies or organizations shall comply with the labor law.

BAR ASSOCIATION

1. A bar association is a socio-professional organization of lawyers in a province or centrally run city, having the legal person status, its own seal and bank account and operating on the principle of self-financing with revenues from membership fees, contributions of members and other lawful revenue sources.

2. A bar association may be set up in a province or centrally run city where exist three or more law practice certificate holders.

3. A bar association has its own charter to govern its internal relations.

4. Members of a bar association are lawyers.

The rights and obligations of members of a bar association are provided in its charter.

TASKS AND POWERS OF A BAR ASSOCIATION

1. To represent lawyers in professional practice and protect their legitimate rights and interests.

2. To supervise and coordinate with bar associations in other localities in supervising the observance of law, rules of professional ethics and conducts of member lawyers, lawyers practicing law in law-practicing organizations and locally based branches of law-practicing organizations; to discipline lawyers.

3. To supervise and coordinate with bar associations in other localities in supervising the operations of law-practicing organizations and their branches and transaction offices; to request law-practicing organizations to stop law-breaking acts and request competent state agencies to handle those acts.

4. To organize the registration of probationary lawyers and supervise them.

5. To receive dossiers of application for law practice certificates and request the Justice Ministry to grant those certificates.

6. To organize the registration of participation in the bar association; to organize the transfer and reception of lawyers; to request the national lawyers' organization to grant lawyer's cards.

7. To assign law-practicing organizations to nominate lawyers or directly nominate lawyers who practice law individually to participate in legal proceedings at the request of legal proceeding-conducting agencies.

8. To conciliate disputes between probationary lawyers, lawyers and law-practicing organizations; between clients and law-practicing organizations or lawyers.

9. To settle complaints and denunciations according to its competence.

10. To sum up and exchange experience, provide professional training and fostering and take other measures to raise professional skills of lawyers.

11. To gather and report lawyers' thoughts, aspirations, opinions and proposals.

12. To make arrangement for lawyers to participate in law dissemination and education.

13. To report to the national lawyers' organization on its organization and operation.

14. To send to the Justice Ministry and the provincial/municipal People's Committee its resolutions and decisions in accordance with law and upon request.

NATIONAL LAWYERS' ORGANIZATION

1. The national lawyers' organization is a socio-professional organization of lawyers nationwide, which represents lawyers and bar associations; has the legal person status, its own seal and bank account; and operates on the principle of self-financing with membership fee revenues, contributions of members and other lawful revenue sources.

Members of the national lawyers' organization are bar associations and lawyers. Lawyers participate in the national lawyers' organization through bar associations which they have joined.

2. The national lawyers' organization has its own charter.

The rights and obligations of members of the national lawyers' organization are provided for in its charter.

TASKS AND POWERS OF THE NATIONAL LAWYERS' ORGANIZATION

1. To represent and protect the legitimate rights and interests of lawyers and bar associations nationwide.

2. To issue and oversee the observance of the rules of professional ethics and conducts by lawyers.

3. To coordinate with the Justice Ministry in issuing the Regulation on lawyers' probation and in training lawyers and examining lawyers' probation results.

4. To organize regular refresher courses on legal knowledge and professional skills for lawyers.

5. To organize reviews and exchange of professional experience among lawyers throughout the country.

6. To provide the uniform model for lawyers participating in court sessions and the form of lawyer's card; to grant, renew and withdraw lawyer's cards.

7. To provide for exemption from and reduction of remunerations for, and pro bono legal aid provided by, lawyers, the resolution of disputes over remunerations and expenses for lawyers.

8. To set lawyer's probation charges and bar associations' participation and membership fees.

9. To settle complaints and denunciations according to its competence.

10. To gather, report lawyers' thoughts, aspirations, opinions and proposals.

11. To join in law-making and jurisprudent research activities as well as in law dissemination and education.

12. To enter in international cooperation in relation to lawyers.

13. To send its resolutions and decisions to the Justice Ministry in accordance with law and upon request.

DISCIPLINE OF LAWYERS

1. Lawyers who violate the provisions of Law on lawyers, charters, rules of professional ethics and conducts and other regulations of socio-professional organizations of lawyers shall, depending on the nature and severity of their violations, be subject to one of the following disciplinary forms:

a/ Reprimand;

b/ Caution;

c/ Suspension of the membership of a bar association for between 6 and 24 months;

d/ Deletion of their names from the list of a bar association.

2. The discipline of lawyers shall be considered and decided by the managing boards of bar associations at the request of their commendation and disciplinary councils.

3. When a lawyer is disciplined in the form of having his/her name deleted from the list of lawyers of a bar association, the bar association shall notify such in writing to the provincial/municipal Justice Service and request the Justice Ministry to withdraw his/her law-practice certificate, and request the national lawyers' organization to withdraw his/her lawyer's card.

COMPLAINT ABOUT DISCIPLINARY DECISIONS AGAINST LAWYERS

1. A lawyer is entitled to complain about a disciplinary decision against him/her which is issued by the managing board of a bar association.

The executive board of the national lawyers' organization is competent to settle complaints against disciplinary decisions of the managing boards of bar associations.

2. When disagreeing with a complaint-settling decision of the executive board of the national lawyers' organization, a lawyer may further lodge a complaint with the Justice Ministry. The time limit for the Justice Minister to settle a complaint is 30 days after the receipt of that complaint.

COMPLAINT ABOUT DECISIONS OR ACTS OF THE MANAGING BOARDS OF BAR ASSOCIATIONS OR BODIES OF THE NATIONAL LAWYERS' ORGANIZATION

1. If having grounds to believe that decisions or acts of the managing boards of bar associations infringe upon their legitimate rights or interests, individuals and organizations may complain about those decisions or acts.

The executive board of the national lawyers' organization is competent to settle complaints about decisions and acts of the managing boards of bar associations.

2. If having grounds to believe that decisions or acts of bodies of the national lawyers' organization infringe upon their legitimate rights or interests, individuals and organizations may complain about those decisions or acts.

The executive board of the national lawyers' organization is competent to settle complaints about decisions or acts of the organization's bodies.

SETTLEMENT OF DISPUTES

When disputes between clients, lawyers and law-practicing organizations arise in relation to law-practice activities, the managing boards of bar associations shall settle those disputes.

HANDLING OF VIOLATIONS OF LAWYERS

Lawyers who violate the provisions of Law on lawyers shall, apart from being disciplined, be administratively handled or examined for penal liability, depending on the nature and severity of their violations; if causing damage, they shall pay compensation in accordance with law.

HANDLING OF ACTS OF INFRINGING UPON LEGITIMATE RIGHTS AND INTERESTS OF LAWYERS AND LAW-PRACTICING ORGANIZATIONS

Persons holding positions or powers who commit acts of infringing upon legitimate rights and interests of lawyers or law-practicing organizations or obstructing lawyers or law-practicing organizations from exercising their rights and/or performing their duties shall, depending on the nature and severity of their violations, be disciplined or examined for penal liability in accordance with law.

HANDLING OF VIOLATIONS OF INDIVIDUALS AND ORGANIZATIONS THAT ILLEGALLY PRACTICE LAW

1. Individuals who are unqualified but still practice law in any form shall be forced to stop their violation acts, be fined according to the law on handling of administrative violations or examined for penal liability; if causing damage, they shall pay compensation in accordance with law.

2. Organizations which practice law in any form though failing to satisfy the relevant conditions shall be forced to stop their violations and be handled in accordance with the law on handling of administrative violations; if causing damage, they shall pay compensation in accordance with law.

Conclusion

Thank you again for downloading this book on *"LAW ON LAWYERS: Essential Legal Terms Explained You Need To Know About Law on Lawyers!"* and reading all the way to the end. I'm extremely grateful.

If you know of anyone else who may benefit from the informative legal words presented in this book, please help me inform them of this book. I would greatly appreciate it.

Finally, if you enjoyed this book and feel that it has added value to your study or career in any way, please take a couple of minutes to share your thoughts and post a REVIEW on Amazon. Your feedback will help me to continue to write the kind of Kindle books that helps you get results. Furthermore, if you write a simple REVIEW with positive words for this book on Amazon, you can help hundreds or perhaps thousands of other readers who may want to enhance their legal vocabulary have a chance getting what they need. Like you, they worked hard for every penny they spend on books. With the information and recommendation you provide, they would be more likely to take action right away. We really look forward to reading your review.

Thanks again for your support and good luck!

If you enjoy my book, please write a POSITIVE REVIEW on amazon.

-- Dr. Peter Johnson --

Check Out Other Books

Go here to check out other related books that might interest you:

Legal Terminology And Phrases: Essential Legal Terms Explained You Need To Know About Crimes, Penalty And Criminal Procedure

http://www.amazon.com/dp/B01L5EB54Y

LAW ON INTELLECTUAL PROPERTY: Essential Legal Terms Explained You Need To Know About Trademarks, Copyrights, Patents, and Trade Secrets!

https://www.amazon.com/dp/B07PFP3MDY

COMPANY LAW: Mastering Essential Legal Terms Explained About Limited Liability Companies, Joint-Stock Companies, Partnership, Private Enterprises, And Groups of Companies!

https://www.amazon.com/dp/B07P2PRVMJ

TAX LAW: Essential Legal Terms Explained You Need To Know About Types of Tax Law!

https://www.amazon.com/dp/B07PH1L3RS

INVESTMENT LAW: Essential Legal Terms Explained You Need To Know About Law On Investment!

https://www.amazon.com/dp/B07P79D925

LABOR LAW: Essential Legal Terms Explained You Need To Know About Law On Labor!

https://www.amazon.com/dp/B07PFD2CML

CIVIL LAW: Mastering Essential Legal Terms Explained About Civil Rights, Guardianship, Civil Transactions, Civil Obligations, Civil Liability, Civil Contracts And Civil Procedure!

https://www.amazon.com/dp/B07P5GS8LD

Legal Vocabulary In Use: Master 600+ Essential Legal Terms And Phrases Explained In 10 Minutes A Day

http://www.amazon.com/dp/B01L0FKXPU

Civil Law Vocabulary In Use: Master 350+ Essential Civil Law Terms And Phrases Explained With Examples In 10 Minutes A Day.

https://www.amazon.com/dp/B0781TQWGV

Criminal Law Vocabulary In Use: Master 400+ Essential Criminal Law Terms And Phrases Explained With Examples In 10 Minutes A Day.

https://www.amazon.com/dp/B078KLR51Z

Administrative And Tax Law In Use : Master 300+ Administrative And Tax Law Terms And Phrases Explained With Examples In 10 Minutes A Day.

https://www.amazon.com/dp/B07JMD546J

Productivity Secrets For Students: The Ultimate Guide To Improve Your Mental Concentration, Kill Procrastination, Boost Memory And Maximize Productivity In Study

http://www.amazon.com/dp/B01JS52UT6

Shortcut To Ielts Writing: The Ultimate Guide To Immediately Increase Your Ielts Writing Scores

http://www.amazon.com/dp/B01JV7EQGG

www.ingramcontent.com/pod-product-compliance
Lightning Source LLC
Chambersburg PA
CBHW030728180526
45157CB00008BA/3088

Thank you again for purchasing this book on "LAW ON LAWYERS. Essential Legal Terms Explained You Need To Know About Law on Lawyers!" and reading all the way to the end. I'm extremely grateful

"As the author of the book, I promise this book will be an invaluable source of legal reference for professionals, international lawyers, law students, business professionals and anyone else who want to improve their use of legal terminology, succinct clarification of legal terms and have a better understanding of law on lawyers. All legal terms and phrases are well written and explained clearly in plain English."